Desert Food Chains

Louise and Richard Spilsbury

Heinemann
LIBRARY

www.heinemann.co.uk/library
Visit our website to find out more information about Heinemann Library books.

To order:
 Phone 44 (0) 1865 888066
 Send a fax to 44 (0) 1865 314091
 Visit the Heinemann Bookshop at www.heinemann.co.uk/library to browse our catalogue and order online.

First published in Great Britain by Heinemann Library, Halley Court, Jordan Hill, Oxford OX2 8EJ, part of Harcourt Education. Heinemann is a registered trademark of Harcourt Education Ltd.

Editorial: Sarah Eason and Kathy Peltan
Design: Jo Hinton-Malivoire and AMR
Illustration: Words and Publications
Picture Research: Ruth Blair and Ginny Stroud-Lewis
Production: Camilla Smith

Originated by Ambassador Litho Ltd
Printed in China by WKT Company Limited.

The paper used to print this book comes from sustainable resources

ISBN 0 431 11903 1 (hardback)
08 07 06 05 04
10 9 8 7 6 5 4 3 2 1

ISBN 0 431 11910 4 (paperback)
09 08 07 06 05
10 9 8 7 6 5 4 3 2 1

British Library Cataloguing in Publication Data
Spilsbury, Louise and Richard
Food Chains: Deserts
577.5'416

A full catalogue record for this book is available from the British Library.

Acknowledgements
The Publishers would like to thank the following for permission to reproduce photographs: Alamy pp. **5**, **14**, **25**; Corbis pp. **7** (Martin B. Withers/Frank Lane Picture Agency), **8** (Michael & Patricia Fogden), **15** (Theo Allofs), **17** (Nigel J. Dennis/Gallo Images), **22** (James Marshall), **23** (Craig Aurness), **26** (Paul A. Souders), p. **18**; FLPA/Minden Pictures p. **24** (Frans Lanting); Getty Images/Photodisc p. **27**; NHPA p. **13** (Stephen Dalton), p. **10**; SPL pp. **11** (Alex Bartel), **12** (Peter Chadwick); Still Pictures p. **16** (Wyman Meinzer).

Cover photograph of a lizard eating an insect reproduced with permission of Bruce Coleman.

The Publishers would like to thank Michael Scott for his assistance in the preparation of this book.

Contents

Words in bold, **like this**, are explained in the Glossary.

What is a desert food web?

All living things need food to live and grow. Most **organisms** feed on other living things. For example, in a desert a mouse that feeds on seeds might be eaten by a snake. A food web is a network of living things that feed on each other in a certain **habitat**.

If you draw lines between each of the organisms that eat each other you create a food web diagram. The arrows lead from the food to the animal that eats it.

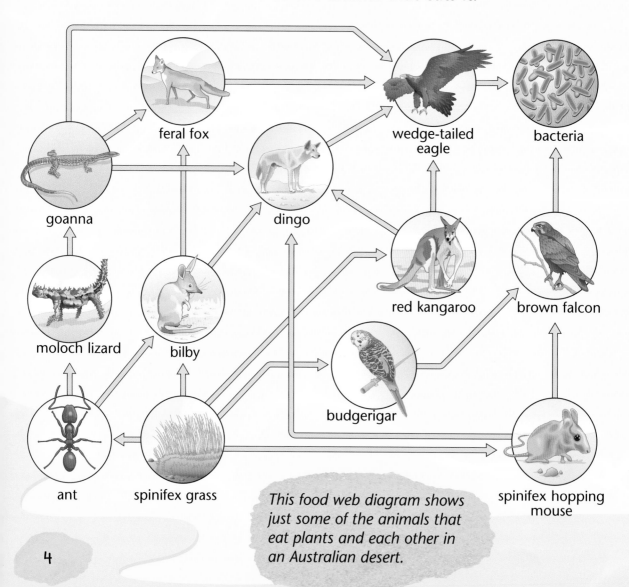

feral fox

wedge-tailed eagle

bacteria

goanna

dingo

moloch lizard

bilby

red kangaroo

brown falcon

budgerigar

ant

spinifex grass

spinifex hopping mouse

This food web diagram shows just some of the animals that eat plants and each other in an Australian desert.

What are desert habitats like?

Most people imagine all deserts to be vast, dry expanses of sand. Although some deserts are sandy, many are stony or scattered with tall rocks. All deserts are very dry. Some get no rain for months or years at a time. Others get regular light rains, but over a year this adds up to very little. Others have more regular rainfall. Many are burning hot in the daytime and freezing cold at night. Because deserts are such harsh places to live, fewer plants and animals are found here than in most other habitats. However, deserts still contain many different food webs and chains to explore.

This area in California, USA, is called Death Valley. Although it is hard for people to live here, this hot desert is home to a wide range of wildlife.

What is a desert food chain?

A food chain diagram shows the **organisms** that eat each other within a **habitat** as links in a single chain. It presents one of many possible routes that food and **energy** can take from one plant or animal to another. A food chain goes from link to link in a single straight line, from food to feeder to other feeders.

Most organisms are part of more than one food chain because they eat more than one kind of food. For example, snakes eat both mice and lizards. Eating more than one kind of food is good for living things. If an animal relied on only one food source, and that food ran out, the animal would starve.

This is an Australian desert food chain. It shows how energy is passed from one link in the food chain to another.

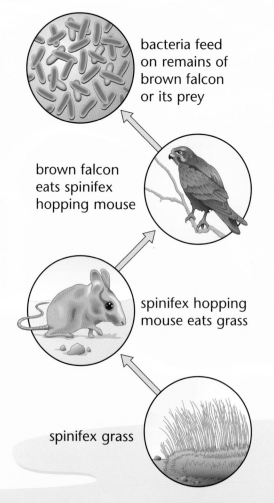

bacteria feed on remains of brown falcon or its prey

brown falcon eats spinifex hopping mouse

spinifex hopping mouse eats grass

spinifex grass

Starting the chain

The Sun is the source of energy for all living things on Earth. Plants capture this energy in their leaves and use it to make their own food in the process called **photosynthesis**. The sugary food a plant makes is a way of storing energy. This food, along with **nutrients** a plant takes up through its roots, allows it to grow and make new plants.

Animals cannot get energy from the Sun – they get the energy they need from food. Some animals eat plant parts. In desert habitats, for example, desert bats eat **nectar** from cactus flowers and many **rodents** eat desert grass seeds. Other animals get energy by eating plant-eaters or other meat-eaters. This is how energy flows through the food chain and through the habitat.

Like other green plants, euphorbia cactuses in the Namib Desert, Africa do not need to eat food – they can make it themselves using energy from the Sun.

Making the chain

The first link in a food chain is a plant. In food chains and webs we call plants **producers**, because they produce (make) food. Animals are called **consumers** because they consume (eat) other organisms to get energy.

Primary consumers eat the producers. **Herbivores** are plant-eating animals that get their energy from eating plant parts, such as seeds, berries or leaves. Herbivores are therefore primary consumers. Animals that eat primary consumers are known as **secondary consumers**. Those that eat only animals are called **carnivores**. Secondary consumers that eat plants as well as other animals are called **omnivores**. Each animal in a chain takes some energy out of it. That is why there are always more producers than consumers.

Peringuey's adders live in desert areas in southern Africa. This one has caught a lizard, so it is a carnivore and a secondary consumer.

More links in the chain

Scavengers are also secondary consumers. A scavenger is an animal that eats the remains of dead animals. In desert habitats, lappet-faced vultures are scavengers.

Decomposers are the last link in a food chain or web. They include insects and organisms such as **bacteria** and **fungi**. They feed on waste and dead plants and animals to get nutrients. Some of these nutrients wash into the soil. When plants take them in through their roots and use them to grow, the food chain begins again.

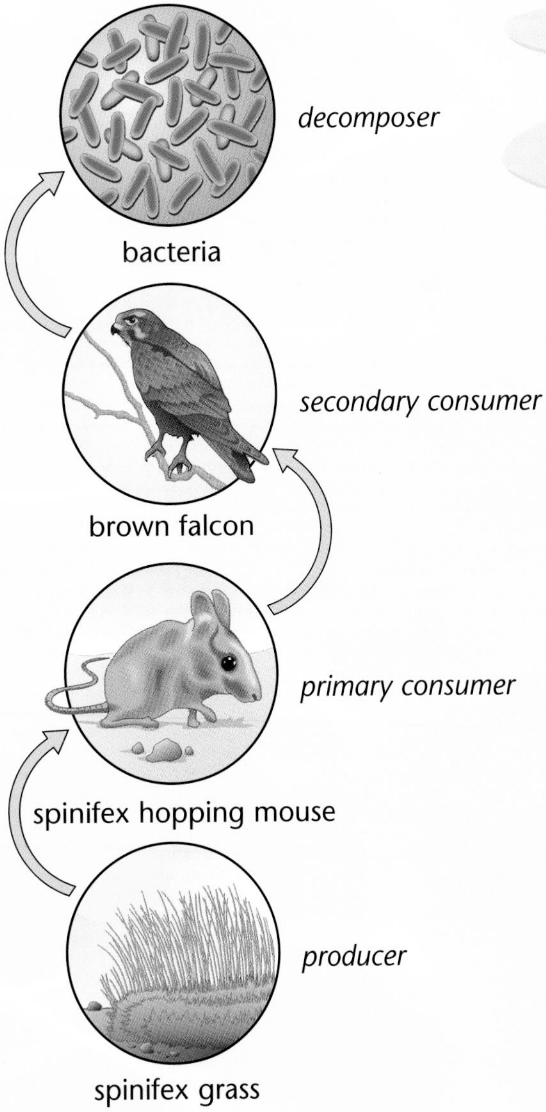

decomposer

bacteria

secondary consumer

brown falcon

primary consumer

spinifex hopping mouse

This diagram shows the movement of energy from producer to consumer and decomposer in an Australian desert food chain.

producer

spinifex grass

Breaking the chain

As all living things are linked together in food webs, a change in one part of the web can affect plants and animals elsewhere in the web. Indeed, if some organisms in a food web die out, it can be disastrous for others.

Sometimes natural events damage a desert food web. If plants die, primary consumers that usually feed on the seeds and flowers these plants produce may die. Then, the animals that feed on those herbivores may also die. In Australian deserts, extra long periods of **drought** can cause plants to shrivel up and die. Immense numbers of seed-eating rodents then seek food on farms, damaging crop fields and grain stores. When grain is lost, human and livestock food chains and webs are affected!

Rats use their sharp, strong front teeth to bite through sacks to eat stored grain.

Which producers live in deserts?

In deserts, as in all **habitats**, plants are the **producers**. Their seeds, flowers, fruits, leaves, roots and juicy stems provide food for desert animals. However, even in deserts with some grasses and trees, plant life is **sparse**. What desert plants there are have special **adaptations** to cope with the extreme conditions.

Cacti are the most famous desert plants. They do not have leaves because plants lose water through their leaves. Cacti use their green stems for **photosynthesis** instead. They are dotted with sharp thorns to make it harder for animals to eat them and get their water stores. Many cactus stems can expand to store water. Other desert plants, such as the agave, store water in thick juicy leaves.

decomposer
bacteria

secondary consumer
brown falcon

primary consumer
spinifex hopping mouse

producer
spinifex grass

Saguaro cacti are found in the desert areas of Mexico and southern USA. They can grow to over 15 metres (nearly 50 feet) and live for 200 years.

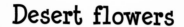

Desert flowers

Some desert flowering plants only live for one year. When rain finally falls, seeds grow, into plants that flower and die in a very short time. The flowers produce more small hard seeds, which are tough enough to survive until the next rains come. Because many desert plants are covered with thorns and are difficult to eat, plant seeds are a vital food for many desert **herbivores**.

When rain falls in Namaqualand, South Africa, seeds that have lain dormant (not active) in the ground for years burst into life and carpet the desert floor with colourful flowers, like these daisies.

Breaking the chain: producers

If a producer is removed from a food chain it can have a disastrous effect on other **organisms** in that habitat. In some deserts, such as the Sonoran in the USA and Mexico, people are digging up cacti to sell to plant collectors. The giant saguaro is especially popular. This takes food from animals that feed on the cactus flowers, fruits and seeds.

Which primary consumers live in deserts?

Primary consumers are animals that eat plants. In deserts they get **energy**, **nutrients** and most of their water from plants. Many desert **herbivores** are small. They hide in **burrows** or under rocks to avoid the heat during the day and feed at night.

Insects such as grasshoppers and beetles have hard, horny mouthparts to help them chew large amounts of leaves. Many **species** of small **rodents**, including kangaroo rats, jerboas and mice eat seeds. Desert hamsters cram seeds into their cheek pouches and store them in their underground burrows. Desert tortoises are protected from the Sun by their hard shells as they search for grasses and cacti fruit to eat. After the rains, many rodents, rabbits and birds eat all the seedlings they can find, to feed up before the dry weather returns.

decomposer
bacteria

secondary consumer
brown falcon

primary consumer
spinifex hopping mouse

producer
spinifex grass

In years when food is scarce in the desert, locusts may form huge swarms and fly across the countryside eating farm crops.

This one-humped dromedary camel mainly feeds on plants, but it also eats remains of dead animals, dried up by the summer heat.

Desert birds and bats

Sandgrouse are desert birds that are **camouflaged** by their mottled brown feathers as they search the ground for seeds to eat. The long-eared bat uses its long tongue to gather up **nectar** and **pollen** from cactus flowers.

Large desert herbivores

Some desert herbivores are large **mammals**. They can walk on sand without sinking into it because they have broad feet that spread their weight. The scimitar-horned oryx is about 2 metres long, but its curving horns can be 1 metre long! Camels are bigger and coated in shaggy hair. Both animals feed on plants such as coarse grasses and thorny shrubs. If camels cannot find much food, they can live off the fat stored inside humps on their backs.

Which secondary consumers live in deserts?

Secondary consumers eat other animals. Many secondary consumers in deserts eat the numerous insects that live in the soil or sand and under plants. The moloch lizard is small, with sharp spines all over its body. It can eat up to 2500 ants a day, catching them on its tongue! Scorpions use their stinging tails to catch insect **prey**. Tarantulas are desert spiders that can be as big as your hand. They hunt insects, other spiders and lizards. Rattlesnakes bite small **mammals**, birds and lizards with fangs that inject **venom**, then they swallow their victims whole.

decomposer

bacteria

secondary consumer

brown falcon

primary consumer

spinifex hopping mouse

producer

spinifex grass

Scorpions have a deadly sting in their tail, but meerkats are not affected by their poison and can eat them without being harmed.

Desert birds

The roadrunner is a speedy desert bird that can catch and eat fast-moving rattlesnakes. It also eats insects, scorpions, lizards, **rodents** and other birds. Hawks, eagles and falcons hunt for small animals during the day and owls hunt them at night. Scrawny-necked vultures fly high in the air and swoop down when they spot a dead animal.

Desert dogs

Several kinds of wild dogs live in deserts. The fennec fox has large ears that help it hear prey animals such as insects, rodents and lizards in the dark. Jackals, such as the black-backed jackal, are **omnivores**. They eat small animals, grasses and fruits, and also scavenge chunks of flesh from dead animals.

The roadrunner is one of the few animals that eats poisonous snakes like this copperhead snake. It catches the snake by the tail, beats its head against the ground until it is dead and then swallows it whole.

Which decomposers live in deserts?

Decomposers are **organisms** that rot down waste and dead plants and animals. They play a vital role in the health of a food chain or web. Without them, dead organisms would just pile up in a **habitat** and few **nutrients** would be returned to the soil for new food chains to begin.

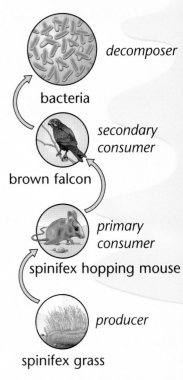

decomposer

bacteria

secondary consumer

brown falcon

primary consumer

spinifex hopping mouse

producer

spinifex grass

Bacteria in the desert

Many decomposers, including **fungi**, thrive in moist conditions so deserts are too dry for them. **Bacteria** are the major decomposers in deserts. They are so small they can only be seen under a microscope, and so light they can float through the air. They live in large numbers in water, soil and sand and on dead plants and animals. They feed by releasing chemicals into dead animals or plants to break them down into liquid nutrients. The bacteria **absorb** some of these nutrients as food. The rest wash into the ground.

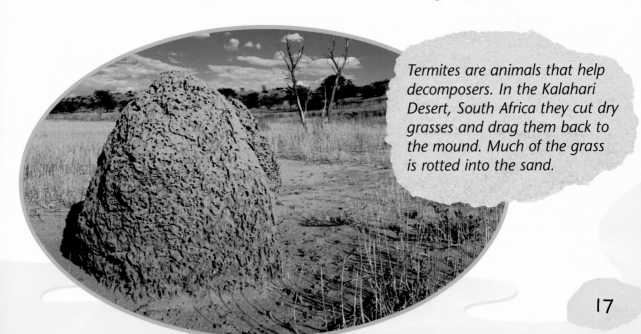

Termites are animals that help decomposers. In the Kalahari Desert, South Africa they cut dry grasses and drag them back to the mound. Much of the grass is rotted into the sand.

17

Animals that help decomposers

The main animals that help decomposers in deserts are insects. Sand termites are ant-like insects with strong jaws for crunching off pieces of plants. They carry these pieces underground, ready for the other members of their large colony (group) to eat. Termites eat some of the plant pieces and bacteria rot the rest, returning some nutrients to the desert soils and sands.

Some insects, such as silver-backed scarab beetles, eat the **dung** of other animals. When they digest waste to release nutrients for themselves, they also put some nutrients back into the soil in the habitat. Some species of ants remove tiny pieces of flesh from **carrion** to carry back to their nest. Other insects, such as flies and carrion beetles, lay eggs on dead animal remains. The **larvae** (young) that hatch out feed on the rotting carcass and so help to break it down.

These silver-backed scarab beetles are feeding on elephant dung in Zimbabwe, Africa.

How are desert food chains different in different places?

Food chains and webs can be very different from one desert to another desert. These are three important desert habitats from around the world.

The Sahara Desert

The Sahara Desert in North Africa is the largest desert in the world, covering an area the size of the USA. Much of it is rock and sand, but grasses, thorny shrubs and trees grow in places and food chains spring from these **producers**.

The fat-tailed jerboa eats seeds, leaves and insects such as crickets. It stores fat in its tail for the winter. The fennec fox uses its huge ears to keep cool during the day. At night they help the fox find insects lizards and **rodents** to eat. The desert horned viper also hunts for **rodents** at night injecting **venom** into them with its long fangs. The sand cat digs up rodents that hide in the sand, but also eats snakes such as the viper.

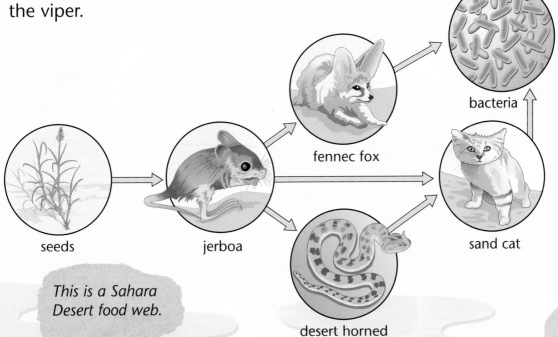

bacteria

fennec fox

seeds   jerboa   sand cat

This is a Sahara Desert food web.

desert horned viper

The Namib Desert

The Namib Desert in south-west Africa lies between the Kalahari Desert and the Atlantic Ocean. It contains the tallest sand dunes in the world at over 300 metres!

The grasses that grow on the dunes are eaten by a variety of insects, such as termites, crickets and the small, black and fast-running tok-tokkie beetles. Grant's golden moles eat some of these insects. These blind **mammals** live underground and tunnel quickly through sand to catch their **prey**. Desert chameleons are insect-eating lizards that can change their colour to match almost any part of the desert. Hungry sidewinder snakes travel swiftly across hot sand using a sideways S-shaped movement to catch lizards. Brown hyenas sometimes hunt small mammals but mostly feed on **carrion**, ostrich eggs and fruits.

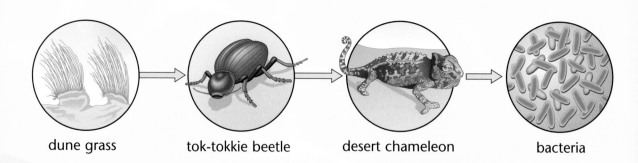

| dune grass | tok-tokkie beetle | desert chameleon | bacteria |

This is a food chain from the Namib Desert in south-west Africa.

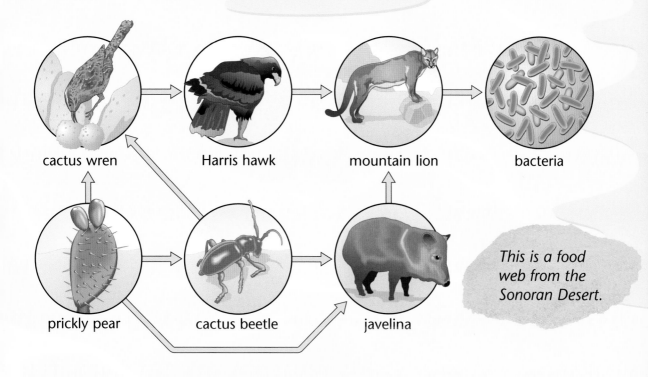

cactus wren · Harris hawk · mountain lion · bacteria

prickly pear · cactus beetle · javelina

This is a food web from the Sonoran Desert.

The Sonoran Desert

The Sonoran Desert covers about 300,000 square kilometres in the USA and Mexico. Many of the producers here are cacti, such as saguaro and prickly pear. Prickly pears grow close to the ground where javelinas, animals that look like small, hairy pigs, can reach their juicy oval fruits. Fruits that fall to the ground are eaten by cactus beetles. The small cactus wren eats these insects as well as fruits, and is eaten in turn by the Harris hawk, a **bird of prey**.

The clown beetle stands on its head and makes a smelly fluid that helps to repel **predators**. It is eaten by the grasshopper mouse, which pushes the end of the beetle into the sand to stop the smell! Owls, coyotes, foxes and snakes are the grasshopper mouse's most common predators.

What happens to a food web when a food chain breaks down?

The living things in a **habitat**, their surroundings and the way their lives are linked are known as an **ecosystem**. When even one link in a food chain or web is affected it can put the entire ecosystem out of balance. Many desert ecosystems are under threat because of things people do.

Habitat destruction

People move into desert habitats for different reasons. Some search for oil and gas beneath the land. When companies dig deep mines to extract oil or gas, the waste can poison land near by. Mining companies also use a lot of water, which can reduce the amount of this precious resource available for wildlife.

In many areas, people are taking over desert land to build towns. These houses outside Las Vegas cover many square kilometres of the Nevada Desert in the USA.

In this area of Tanzania, East Africa, overgrazing has damaged the desert plant life.

Overgrazing

Another major problem is overgrazing. When herds of goats and other farm livestock on the edges of deserts eat too many desert plants they destroy vital **producers** in the food chain. When plants die, any fertile soil is blown away leaving only dusty land on which very little can grow.

Breaking the chain: unwanted additions

Food chains and webs can be harmed if a new **organism** is introduced to their habitat. For example, in some parts of the Mojave Desert in the USA, overgrazing by farm animals has destroyed **native** plants and new weed **species** have taken over. Desert tortoises happily eat these weeds too, but unlike the native plants the weeds burn easily. When natural fires occur, the tortoises' supply of food can be wiped out, putting their lives at serious risk.

Other human activities

People affect and damage desert ecosystems in a number of other ways. For example, tourists and visitors often like to drive off-road over wide expanses of wild desert and if they are not careful they can crush plants and disturb wildlife. In Mexico, desert bat populations are threatened by tourism. When tourists visit caves they disturb the places where bats rest during the day. The bats are then less likely to **breed** there.

Wars in desert regions, such as Iraq, destroy habitats as well as lives. The destruction of oil wells in wars results in huge lakes of oil that **pollute** underground water supplies. Some desert ecosystems, such as parts of the Mojave Desert in the USA, are wrecked when armies train for war.

Off-road events like this motocross race in California, USA can damage desert plants and break the food chain.

How can we protect desert food chains?

Around the world, many people are working to protect the plants, animals and other **organisms** in desert food chains and webs.

Scientists study **ecosystems** in order to understand them. By studying the lives of organisms in a food chain or web scientists can work out if any are in trouble and why. They can then help decide what needs to be done to protect them. For example, scientists thought that a kind of lizard called the great desert skink was **extinct** in Australian deserts as a result of introduced **predators** such as cats. When some of these skinks were discovered alive, the Australian government started protecting them.

This scientist is taking measurements in the desert of Wahuba, Oman, to show how its sand dunes shift over time.

Conservation in the desert

Conservation organizations are groups of people who work to conserve (protect) **habitats** and the living things within them. Many of these international groups are charities, such as WWF, which rely on **donations** and support from ordinary people to fund their work.

Others are local groups working to protect local habitats. For example, in the Sonoran desert, USA, the Ironwood Alliance is working to conserve ironwood trees. These trees can live for 1500 years. Many new cacti and other desert plants grow up under their shelter and many insects live among their branches. However, the trees are destroyed when habitat is cleared for building or when their wood is used for fuel or carving. Their loss threatens many food chains.

*Uluru National Park in Australia is a desert conservation area. Some areas are protected because they are **sacred** to the **aboriginal** people, and this also protects the wildlife.*

NO CLIMBING — SACRED AREA
TATINTJAWIYA

Research a desert food web

You can research your own desert food chains and webs using information from this and other books or sources on the Internet. You could construct a paper chain, drawing or labelling one organism per link, to form a food chain. If you pin one to a board or wall you could then add more chains to form a food web!

Here are some other things to think about when making desert food chains.

1. What are the main plant **producers** in the desert?
2. Which **primary consumers** feed on them?
3. How do **secondary consumers** find and catch their **prey**?
4. When you have made your chain, think about what would happen to the other organisms if you removed one of the links from it.

Deserts are beautiful and important habitats for many kinds of plants and animals, and must be conserved.

Where are the world's main deserts?

This map shows the location of the main desert **habitats** across the world.

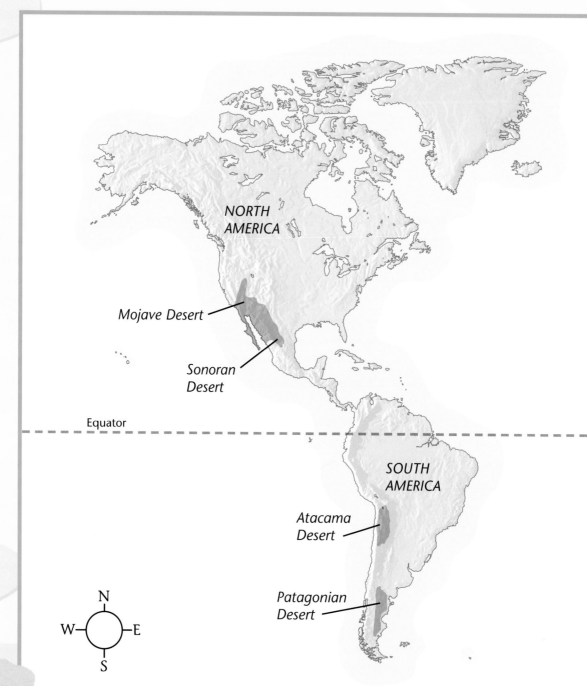

NORTH
AMERICA

Mojave Desert

Sonoran
Desert

Equator

SOUTH
AMERICA

Atacama
Desert

Patagonian
Desert

N
W — E
S

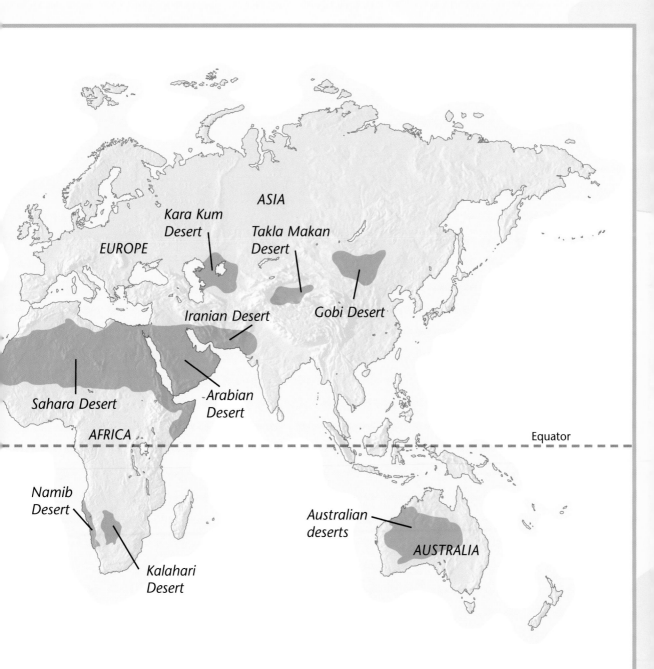

EUROPE

ASIA

Kara Kum
Desert

Takla Makan
Desert

Iranian Desert

Gobi Desert

Sahara Desert

Arabian
Desert

AFRICA

Equator

Namib
Desert

Australian
deserts

AUSTRALIA

Kalahari
Desert

Glossary

aboriginal the original people of Australia

absorb take in through the surface of skin, leaves or roots

adaptation features that help organisms live in their habitat, such as ways of storing water in deserts

bacteria (singular bacterium) tiny living decomposers found everywhere

bird of prey bird that hunts animals for food

breed produce young

burrow hole made in the ground by a rabbit or similar animal

camouflage when an animal has colours and patterns that help it blend in with its background

carnivore animal that eats the flesh of another animal

carrion dead and rotting animals

conservation protecting and saving the natural environment

consumers organisms that eat other organisms

decomposers organisms that break down and get nutrients from dead plants and animals and their waste

donation money given as a gift

drought a long period with no rain

dung animal droppings

ecosystem living system made up of all the organisms in an area and their habitat

endangered when a species of plant or animal is in danger of dying out completely

energy power to grow, move and do things

extinct when a species has died out completely

fungi group of decomposer organisms including mushrooms, toadstools and their relatives

habitat place where an organism lives

herbivore animal that eats plants

larvae (singular larva) the young of some insects and other animals

mammals group of animals that feed their babies on milk from their own bodies

native belonging naturally to an area

nectar sugary substance made by plants to attract insects, which eat it

nutrients chemicals that plants and animals need to live

omnivore animal that eats both plants and other animals

organism living thing

photosynthesis process by which plants make their own food using carbon dioxide (a gas in the air), water and energy from sunlight

pollen small grains that are the male parts of a flower. Pollen combines with eggs (female flower parts) to form seeds.

pollination when pollen moves or is carried from the male part of a flower to the female part

pollute allow chemicals or other substances that can damage animal or plant life to escape into water, soil or the air

predators animals that hunt and eat other animals

prey animals that are caught and eaten by predators

primary consumers animals that eat plants

producer organism (plant) that can make its own food

rodents mammals with large gnawing front teeth such as mice and rats

sacred holy, to do with religion

scavengers organisms that feed on dead plants and animals, and waste

secondary consumers animals that eat primary consumers and other secondary consumers

sparse thin, or thinly scattered

species group of organisms that are very similar and can breed together to produce young

venom poison delivered by a sting or bite

Find out more

Books and CD-Roms

Science Answers: Food Chains and Webs, Louise and Richard Spilsbury (Heinemann Library, 2004)

Taking Action: WWF, Louise Spilsbury (Heinemann Library, 2000)

The Life of Plants: Plant Habitats, Louise and Richard Spilsbury (Heinemann Library, 2002)

Food Chains and Webs CD-ROM (Heinemann Library, 2004) has supporting interactive activities and video clips.

Websites

www.desertmuseum.org/kids
The children's section of the Arizona Sonora Desert Museum has lots of facts about plants and animals that live there.

www.pbs.org/sahara/wildlife
There is information here about the wildlife of the Sahara Desert.

www.enchantedlearning.com/biomes/desert
This is about biomes of the world. Click on 'deserts' to find out more about deserts of the world.

Find out more about the conservation work of these organizations at:
www.wwf.org.uk WWF-UK
www.foe.co.uk Friends of the Earth UK
www.wwf.org.au WWF Australia
www.foe.org.au Friends of the Earth Australia

Index

Titles in the *Food Chains and Webs* series include:

Hardback   0 431 11903 1

Hardback   0 431 11905 8

Hardback   0 431 11904 X

Hardback   0 431 11902 3

Hardback   0 431 11901 5

Hardback   0 431 11900 7

Find out about the other titles in this series on our website www.heinemann.co.uk/library